Korean Power!
Korean Play On Words!
A Collection of Korean-English Jokes

Words by Sarah Jaewon Lee

Pictures by Sae Kim

Text Copyright © 2020 by Sarah Jaewon Lee
Illustration Copyright © 2020 by Sae Kim
Editor, Art Direction & Book Design by Naomi Lau | Wildberry Ink

This book may not be reproduced in whole or in part,
in any form or by any means, electronic or mechanical,
including photocopying, recording, or by any
information storage and retrieval system
now known or hereafter invented,
without written persmission from the publisher.

Printed in the USA

ISBN 9780990591597 (Hardback)

Typography: Myanmar MN, Nanum Gothic

Wildberry Ink | Naomi Lau
San Francisco, CA
www.wildberryink.com

Author's Note

Thank you so much for reading our book! I hope you enjoy it. Growing up in the United States, it was hard to find books that taught me both Korean and English, which made me think it must be weird to be bilingual. But I learned that's not true! More than half the people in the world speak more than one language. I hope this book shows you that it's a really awesome and fun skill (dare I say, superPOWer) to have.

Introduction

Korean POWer (POW stands for Play on Words) is a book of Korean and English bilingual jokes. These jokes provide a fun learning tool to expand your Korean-English vocabulary. The question part of the joke will always be in English, and the answer will usually be either: (1) a mix of Korean that also sounds like an English word, (2) Korean words with two meanings (like a "ball" used in sports or "ball" like a party in English), or (3) two different Korean words that sound similar (like "there" and "their" in English).

What do you call a cute baby with no ears?

Answer

Korean/Hangul: 귀없다

Romanization: *Gwee up dah!*

English Translation: "Has no ears!"

Explanation: This phrase sounds like 귀엽다 *gwee yup dah* "cute." This joke could also work with a puppy, a stuffed animal or anything else you think is cute.

What do you get when a bird poops on your head?

Answer

Korean/Hangul: 똥머리

Romanization: *Ttong muh ree*

English Translation: "Bun"

Explanation: This Korean phrase refers to the hair style, but can also be translated literally to 똥 *ttong* "poop" and 머리 *muh ree* "hair/head." According to Namuwiki (https://namu.wiki/똥머리), this word appeared after the 1980s when a hair bun was just translated as "up do" in Korean. The new phrase probably refers to a bun's round shape. Wouldn't you agree that buns kind of look like the poop emoji? If you don't have your own smart device, ask a family member to show you on their phone!

What do you call a big sheet of tissue?

Answer

Korean/Hangul: 휴지

Romanization: *Hyu jee* (Hint: When you pronounce this aloud, what English word does it sound like to you?)

English Translation: "tissue"

Explanation: This word sounds like the English word "huge." Try finding other Korean words that sound like English words. Here's a hint for another joke: The Korean word for "grandma" might remind you of something music related in English.

Where do Australians keep their money?

Answer

Korean/Hangul: 호주머니

Romanization: *Ho ju muh nee*

English Translation: "pocket"

Explanation: If you break this word in half, 호주 *ho ju* by itself means "Australia" and 머니 *muh nee* sounds like English "money;" Extra vocabulary for the curious: 돈 *don* is the Korean word for "money."

What do you call a family joke?

Answer

Korean/Hangul: 가족

Romanization: *ga jok*

English Translation: "family"

Explanation: The first syllable 가 *ga* on its own also means "family," and the second syllable 족 *jok* sounds like English "joke." Extra vocabulary for the curious: 농담 *nong dam* is the Korean word for "joke." Can you try coming up with your own 농담 now?

What do you get after you tell 10,000 jokes?

Answer

Korean/Hangul: 만족

Romanization: *man jok*

English Translation: "satisfaction"

Explanation: 만 *man* by itself means "10,000" and the second syllable 족 *jok* sounds like English "joke." Can you come up with that many jokes?!

Guess what my favorite kind of ramen is?

Answer

Korean/Hangul: 너와함께라면

Romanization: *Nuh wah ham kkeh ra myun*

English Translation: "If I'm with you"

Explanation: The last two syllables 라면 *ra myun* also mean "ramen" in Korean. This phrase could also answer the question "Do you know my favorite time to eat ramen?" In this context, it would mean "whenever I'm with you."

When did the bread and butter go on their first date?

Answer

Korean/Hangul: 발란타인 데이

Romanization: *Balla*-ntine's Day!

English Translation: There's no English translation, because it's not a real word!

Explanation: The first two syllables of this made-up phrase sounds like 발라 *balla* "to spread." The whole phrase sounds like 발렌타인 데이 *bal le tai een deh ee* "Valentine's Day." It is a holiday celebrated annually on February 14th in the United States and other parts of the world to celebrate love.

What is a vampire's favorite drink?

Answer

Korean/Hangul: 코피

Romanization: *ko pee*

English Translation: "Nosebleed"

Explanation: This word sounds like 커피 *kuh pee* "coffee." When a word is borrowed directly from another language like this, it's called a loan word.

What did the bus driver say to the egg?

Answer

Korean/Hangul: 계란

Romanization: *Geh ran*

English Translation: "egg"

Explanation: This word sounds similar to English "get on." For some reason, there's two words for egg in Korean, and the other is 달걀 *dal gyal*. Try using both next time you're eating breakfast!

What did the bus driver say to the tiger?

Answer

Korean/Hangul: 타 이거

Romanization: *ta ee guh*

English Translation: "get on this (bus)"

Explanation: 타 이거 *ta ee guh* sounds like tiger. 호랑이 *ho rang ee* is the Korean word for "tiger."

Why couldn't the penguin cross the road?

Answer

Korean/Hangul: 차가와서

Romanization: *Cha ga wah suh!*

English Translation: "Because a car was coming"

Explanation: This phrase sounds like 차가워서 *cha ga wuh suh* "because it was cold." This joke could also work with a polar bear, a popsicle or anything else you can think of that lives in a cold environment.

What do you call a kiss from a hippopotamus?

Answer

Korean/Hangul: 힙뽀뽀

Romanization: *hip ppo ppo*

English Translation: "hip - kiss"

Explanation: The whole phrase sounds similar to English "hippo," and the last two syllables 뽀뽀 *ppo ppo* means "kiss" in Korean. Extra vocabulary for the curious: 하마 *ha ma* is the Korean word for "hippopotamus." Now go give a 뽀뽀 to your loved ones!

Sarah Jaewon Lee - Author

While having dinner with friends and family one evening, a friend jokingly asked her if she could write books for Asian-American children like his daughter. Just then, Sarah knew she wanted to join the small but growing number of Asian-American authors, while also using her experience in early childhood and linguistics research. Sarah's books will be the result of her lifelong nerdiness combined with her silly personality. She holds a Bachelor of Arts in Linguistics with a minor in Consumer Psychology from the University of Pennsylvania. Sarah's study of language extended to the realms of cognitive science, education, and marketing. She most recently worked at the Bay Area Discovery Museum in Sausalito, California and served on the board of Next Generation Scholars. She currently resides in Nashville, Tennessee while she pursues her PhD in Education at Vanderbilt University. Her family still lives in her childhood home in Marin County, California.

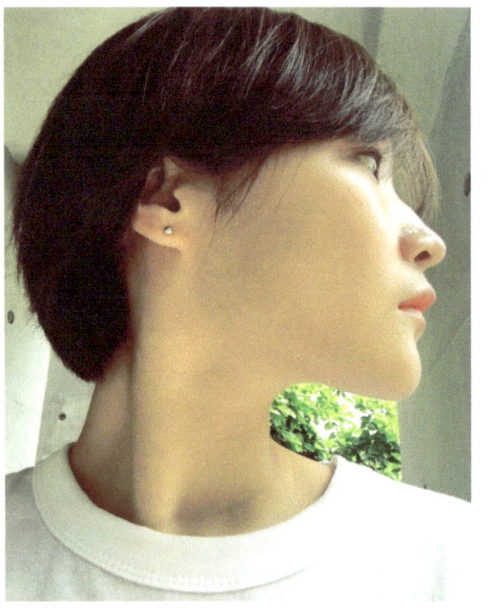

Sae Kim - Illustrator

Sae Kim was born in Korea. She had always dreamt of becoming an artist in the United States. After graduating from high school, she pursued her dreams and moved to the United States, studying character animation. Since graduating and launching her career in the visual effects industry, she has returned to Seoul to continue pursuing her love for the arts. When she's not working, she illustrates by using the strengths of animation. She also enjoys some cake, especially fruit cake. Friends endearingly nicknamed her "Bonobono the Sae Otter," after a curious sea otter anime character who has her likeness. Check out her work at cargocollective.com/saepoula. She holds a Bachelor of Character Animation at California Institute of the Arts and currently works at a visual effects company in Seoul, South Korea.

www.ingramcontent.com/pod-product-compliance
Lightning Source LLC
Chambersburg PA
CBHW040736150426
42811CB00064B/1705